Contents

The game of tennis

Tennis is an energetic sport that involves good **reflexes**. An early form of tennis was played by the ancient Greeks, but it was not until the 19th century that tennis became popular in England. Now it is played all over the world.

Tennis can be played by two or four people. It is played on a court with a net in the middle. The aim of the game is to hit the ball over the net with a racket and to keep the ball in play within the **boundaries** of the court. The game is won by winning points, games and sets (see page 23).

STARTING SPORT

Tennis

Rebecca Hunter

Photography by Chris Fairclough

FRANKLIN WATTS

First published in 2008 by
Franklin Watts
338 Euston Road
London NW1 3BH

Franklin Watts Australia
Level 17/207 Kent Street
Sydney NSW 2000

ISBN: 978 0 7496 7832 6

Dewey classification number: 796.342

A CIP catalogue record for this book is available
from the British Library.

Planning and production by Discovery Books Limited
Editor: Rebecca Hunter
Designer: Ian Winton
Photography: Chris Fairclough
Additional photography: Istockphoto.com: p. 9 top (Bruno Medley); p. 9
middle (Serghei Starus); p. 9 bottom (Richard Stanley); p. 17 top (Graham
Heywood); p. 22 bottom (Joe McDaniel); p. 23 left (David Lee).
Consultant: Justin Layne, CCA qualified coach, former No. 8 British player.

The author, packager and publisher would like to thank the following
people for their participation in this book: Justin Layne, Hamid Hejazi, the
children of Great Shelford Tennis Club and Hereford Cathedral Junior School.

Printed in China

Franklin Watts is a division of Hachette Children's Books,
an Hachette Livre UK company
www.hachettelivre.co.uk

Equipment

To play tennis each player needs a racket and some tennis balls. Tennis balls are made of rubber with a wool fibre covering.

Kit

Tennis clothes should be loose-fitting and comfortable. Tennis players traditionally wear white clothes but coloured kit is becoming more popular.

A hat keeps the sun out of the player's eyes.

T-shirt

Tennis balls

Shorts

Racket

Socks

Training shoes with a good grip

The court

Tennis is played on a court that is 24m long and 11m wide. It is marked with lines that show the players where to stand and where the ball should be played. Across the centre of the court is the net which is 1m high.

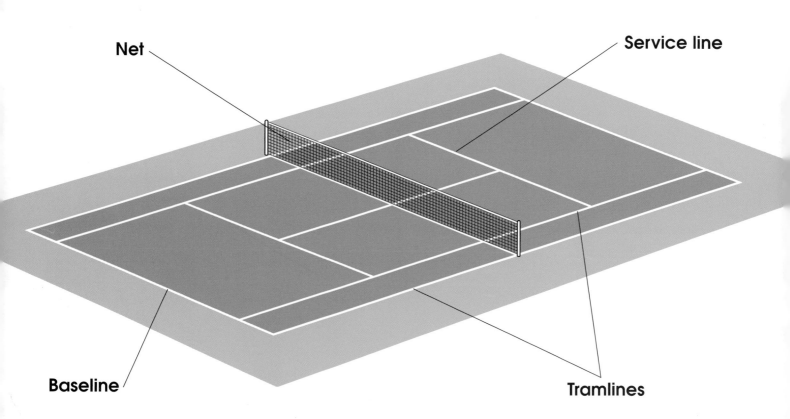

Net

Service line

Baseline

Tramlines

Along each side of the court are pairs of lines called tramlines. The tramline area of the court is only used if four players are playing. The centre of each side has a line across the middle called the service line.

Types of surface

Tennis can be played indoors or outdoors and on several different types of surface. Most outdoor courts are made of a **tarmac**-type material.

Some courts (above) are painted different colours inside and outside the court area. This makes it easier to see if the ball is in or out.

The type of surface affects how quickly the ball bounces. A clay court (left) has a powdery surface. This makes the ball bounce higher but more slowly.

Grass courts make the ball bounce fastest. The most famous grass tennis court in the world is Centre Court at Wimbledon, in London.

Warming up

Before playing a game of tennis, you must do some warming up exercises. These will help loosen and stretch your muscles and joints and will prevent you hurting yourself.

Begin by jogging. This helps warm up your feet and legs.

Dynamic stretches

Dynamic stretches are good for getting muscles ready to work hard. First, stretch your arms above your head. Feel the stretch in your back and arms. Next circle your arms like windmills.

To stretch the muscles in your legs, do some lunges (right). Step forward on one leg bending both knees. Try this a few times with both legs.

Ball skills

Before playing it is good to practise some ball skills.

First bounce the ball with a friend. When you can do this easily, try throwing it to each other.

Now try some ball skills using your racket. Walk along the court lines (below) balancing the ball on your racket. Next try running along without losing the ball.

When you have mastered this, try bouncing the ball on the racket (right) and then try to run while bouncing the ball.

The racket

There are many types of racket. They come in different lengths and with different sized heads. Junior rackets are about 55cm long and are quite light in weight. Test a few rackets and find one that feels right for you before buying.

There are two main grips: the forehand grip and the backhand grip.

Forehand grip

The easiest way to learn the forehand grip is to put your racket on the ground and pick it up! Your hand should be at the end of the racket with your thumb wrapped around the handle.

The 'V' between your finger and thumb should sit on the right edge of the handle. This grip is called the semi-western grip.

Backhand grip

There is an easy method for learning the backhand grip. Put your racket under your non-playing arm and pull it out with the other hand. Your hand will naturally grip the racket in the correct way.

Once you have learned the basic grips, get someone to throw you a few practice balls. First of all, just try to get the ball back over the net. Remember to watch the ball carefully at all times.

Forehand hitting

In tennis you can either hit the ball before it bounces or after one bounce. If you hit it after it bounces it is called a **groundstroke**. There are two types of groundstroke, the forehand drive and the backhand drive. The forehand drive is the stroke you will learn first.

1. As the ball approaches, step forward and swing your racket back.

2. Move forward and bring the racket up to meet the ball. Try to hit the ball at a height between your knee and your shoulder.

3. Hit the ball and follow through with your racket.

Short court practice

Practise your forehand drive (above) with a friend on a short court – that means playing between the service lines. Don't try to play clever shots, just try to return the shots and get a **rally** going.

Backhand hitting

A backhand drive is harder to master than the forehand drive but it can be a very powerful stroke. When you first start playing you will probably want to use two hands on the racket. This is called a double-handed backhand. Tennis players can be right-handed or left-handed. This player on the right is left-handed.

1. Turn your shoulder and feet to the side and swing your racket back behind you.

2. Step forward to meet the ball and swing the racket up.

Single-handed backhands

When you get older and better at tennis you may find it useful to learn to play the backhand stroke with one hand. This allows you to reach much further for wide balls, and can be just as powerful.

3. Push forward with your back foot and hit the ball in front of you.

4. Continue the swing. Then follow through with the racket so that it ends up over your shoulder.

Serving

In a game one player serves and the other receives. To serve, first throw the ball up and over your head. At a high point, hit it hard over the net. A good serve that is impossible to return is called an **ace**, and wins the point.

Stand just behind the **baseline** with your body turned sideways. Hold the ball out in front of you.

1. Throw the ball up in the air and take your racket back and up.

2. Throw your racket over your head and hit the ball hard at the highest point you can reach.

3. Let your racket follow through and bring your back foot forward to keep your balance.

Underarm serve

Younger players who are not ready for an overarm serve, can still play the game by using an underarm serve. Stand behind the baseline and throw the ball up gently. Hit the ball before it bounces.

Returning a serve

You need to be ready and alert to return a good serve. Stand near the back of the court and be ready to run forward. The ball must land the other side of the net on the opposite side of the court to the server. If the ball goes over the service line, the serve is out.

Volleying

A volley is a shot that is played before the ball touches the ground. You will usually use a volley shot when you are standing close to the net – about 2m away. There is less time to hit the ball so you have to be quick and watch the ball carefully.

Unlike the forehand drive, you do not need a big swing of the racket to hit the ball. A volley is a short, sharp punch.

1. Take your racket back at about the level you will hit the ball.

2. Step forward to meet the ball. Your racket should form a 'V' with your arm.

3. Punch the racket forward to hit the ball.

You need a lot of practice
to play a volley shot well so get
someone to throw you some practice balls.

The smash

The smash is a shot that can be played like a volley shot
but usually after the ball has bounced. The smash is a bit
like hitting a serve and if it is a very high ball you may
need to jump. If played well it can be the most powerful
stroke of all and is very difficult to return.

Rules and scoring

There are many rules for tennis but you only need to learn the basic ones to begin with.

Players take it in turns to serve. Each player serves for one game at a time. The person who is serving is allowed two tries. If the first ball goes out or into the net it is called a **fault**. Two bad serves are called a double fault and the opponent wins the point. If a served ball touches the net and is still in, this is called a let. The server is allowed another serve.

As you serve you must keep your feet behind the baseline. If your foot touches or goes over the line (as shown, right) it is called a foot fault.

A ball is counted to be in if any part of it touches the line. This ball (left) would count as in.

Scoring

A player must win four points to win a game. Scoring is like this: 0 (or **love**), 15, 30, 40, game. If the score is 40-40 (or **deuce**), a player must get two points in a row to win the game. You need to win 6 games to win the set and 2 or 3 sets to win the match.

Playing a game

Once you have learned the basic strokes of tennis, how to serve and how to score, you are ready to play a game.

Two players can play a **singles** game, or four players can play a **doubles** game.

Traditionally one of the players spins a racket to see who will serve first. You choose some mark or name on the racket and guess if it will land up or down.

The person who is serving stands behind the baseline (left).

The player who is waiting to receive the ball stands in the **ready position**, like this (right).

In a doubles game each pair should work as a team. You need to work together to win points. A player is usually responsible for a ball on their side of the court, although sometimes the two players may cover the front and back of the court.

The player who is serving announces the score at the end of each point, just before they do their next serve.

At the end of the game it is good manners to shake hands with your opponents and thank them for the game.

Mini Tennis

Mini Tennis is a fun version of tennis for players between four and ten years old. Using smaller equipment, softer balls and smaller courts, Mini Tennis allows young players to develop tennis skills at their own speed.

Mini Tennis has three colours of ball, used at different stages: red, orange and green. Red is the easiest and for the youngest children.

As players progress, the court size and racket size increase, making the game faster. By the green stage, players are ready to play on a full size court with real tennis balls.

Glossary

ace when a player serves the ball and it cannot be returned.

baseline the white line at the back of the court. You stand behind it to serve.

boundaries lines that mark the edges of an area.

deuce when the score in a game is 40-40.

doubles a tennis match played with two pairs of people.

dynamic something that is full of energy and movement.

fault a serve that either goes out or does not go over the net.

groundstroke a stroke that is used to hit the ball once it has bounced.

love the term used when a player has a score of '0' in a game.

rally hitting the ball backwards and forwards between two players without it going out or into the net.

ready position the position you stand in when you are waiting to hit the ball.

reflexes the ability to perform an action.

singles a game of tennis that is played with just two people.

tarmac a material that is usually used for surfacing roads.

Further reading

Tennis: Know Your Sport, Rita Storey, Franklin Watts Ltd, 2007

Tennis School, in association with the Wimbledon Junior Tennis Initiative, Naia Bray-Moffatt, Dorling Kindersley, 2005

How to Play Tennis, Venus and Serena Williams, Dorling Kindersley, 2004

Junior Tennis: A Complete Coaching Manual for the Young Tennis Player, Mark Vale, Barron's Educational Series, 2002

Further information

It is easy to get started in Tennis. To find out more you can contact your local council, a registered club or The Lawn Tennis Association.

The Lawn Tennis Association
The National Tennis Centre
100 Priory Lane
Roehampton
London, SW15 5JQ
Website: www.lta.org.uk

Australian Sports Commission
PO Box 176
Belconnen ACT 2616
Australia
Email:club.development@ausport.gov.au
Website: www.ausport.gov.au

Tennis Australia
Postal Address:
Private Bag 6060
Richmond
Victoria 3121
Australia
Website: www.tennis.com.au

Index